CRAZY-O-METER

I0802809

TEN AWFUL HISTORICAL EVENTS

by E. C. Andrews

BEARPORT PUBLISHING

Bearport Books, an imprint of Bearport Publishing by FlutterBee

Credits
All images are courtesy of Shutterstock.com, unless otherwise specified. With thanks to Getty Images, Thinkstock Photo, and iStockphoto.

Cover and title page, © Antoine Buchet, lightmax84, Romolo Tavani; Background pattern throughout, © topform; 2–3, © Everett Collection; 4–5, © Shutter B Photo, Kovalov Anatolii, Design by William Ludwell Sheppard, Engraving by William James Linton, No restrictions, via Wikimedia Commons; 6–7, © lemono, QatlasMaps, Christopher Hall, Wellcome Library, London, CC BY 4.0 via Wikimedia Commons; 8–9, © NikAndr, John Hayls, Public domain, via Wikimedia Commons, Yale Center for British Art, Public domain, via Wikimedia Commons; 10–11, © Simply Amazing, PaoloBrt, Everett Collection, Francis Godolphin Osbourne Stuart, Public domain, via Wikimedia Commons; 12–13, © The img, Kateryna Upit, lux3000, Iwan Noerjono; 14–15, © akids.photo.graphy, GreenSkyStudio, Everett Collection; 16–17, © Soloma, Darryl Brooks, BlackMac; 18–19, © Everett Collection, ro9drigo; 20–21, © Illustration_Desing, Unidentified painter, CC0, via Wikimedia Commons, Bibliothèque nationale de France, Public domain, via Wikimedia Commons, Museum of the French Revolution, CC BY-SA 4.0 via Wikimedia Commons, santima.studio; 22–23, © Kseniia Gorova, Maria Kuza, WinWin artlab, Nadia Chi, Los Angeles County Museum of Art, Public domain, via Wikimedia Commons.

Bearport Publishing Company Product Development Team
Kayla Eggert, Theresa Emminizer, Kim Jones, Allison Juda, Cole Nelson, Naomi Reich, Steve Scheluchin, Tiana Tran

Library of Congress Cataloging-in-Publication Data is available at www.loc.gov or upon request from the publisher.

ISBN: 979-8-89577-604-9 (hardcover)
ISBN: 979-8-89577-692-6 (ebook)

Bearport Publishing is a division of FlutterBee Education Group.

For more information, write to Bearport Publishing, 3500 American Blvd W, Suite 150, Bloomington, MN 55431.
Printed in the United States of America.

CONTENTS

EXTREMELY AWFUL

History is full of horrible, gory stories. Let's take a look back at some truly awful events. How grim do they get?

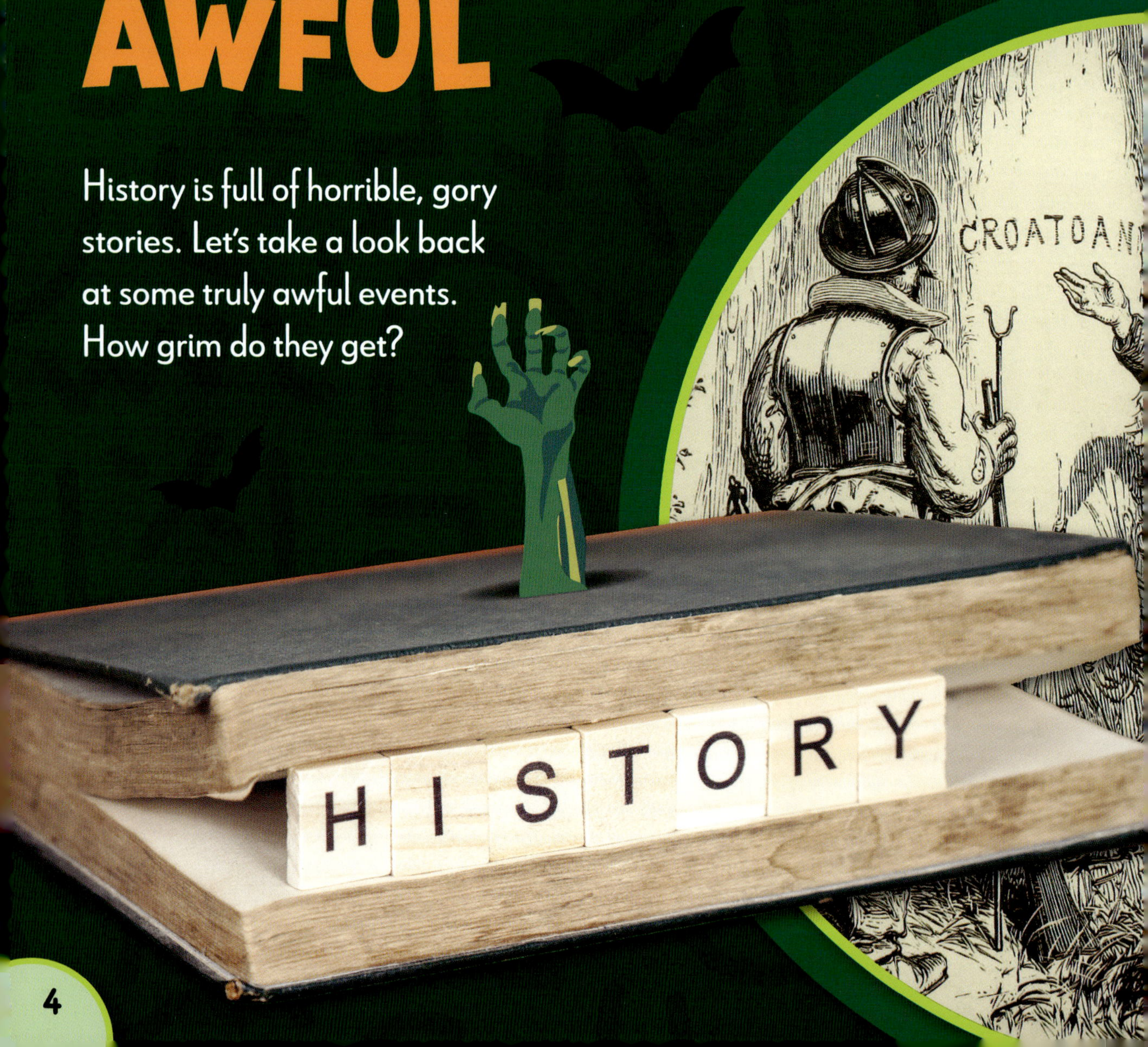

THE LOST COLONY

WHEN: **1590** WHERE: **Roanoke, North Carolina**

How could an entire town vanish? Nobody knows. But one day, every member of the Roanoke Colony disappeared. The only clue was the name of a Native American **tribe** and nearby island, CROATOAN, carved on a post.

Some people think the settlers may have left to join the tribe.

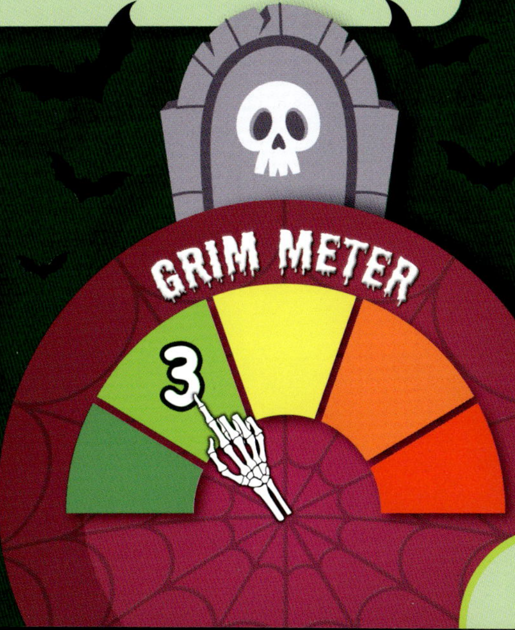

THE DANCING PLAGUE

WHEN: **1518** WHERE: **Strasbourg, France**

In the streets of Europe, one woman started dancing . . . and couldn't stop! Soon, others joined along, dancing with her.

Her dancing party got bigger and bigger. As many as 400 people became affected by this strange **plague**. Stories say that some people danced themselves to death!

The dancing plague lasted for about two months.

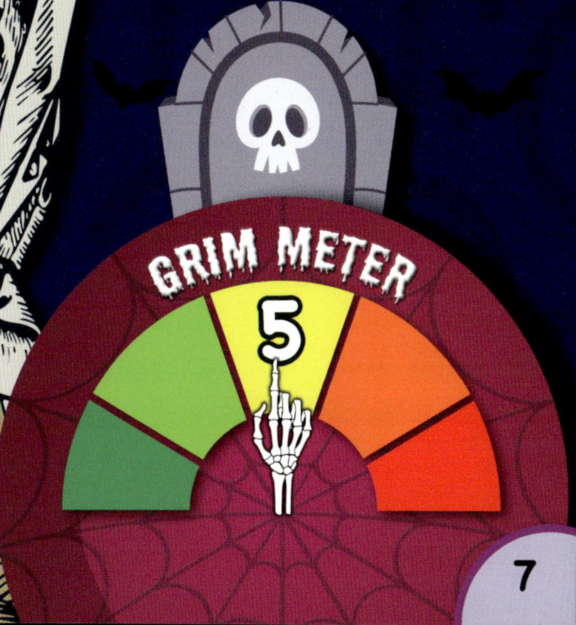

THE GREAT FIRE OF LONDON

WHEN: **1666** WHERE: **London, England**

One fateful day, a bakery in London caught fire. The flames spread and burned down a huge chunk of the city. Over the course of five days, the fire destroyed thousands of wooden houses and buildings.

Luckily, only six people are known to have died. However, there may have been others who were killed but whose bodies were never found.

The writer and politician Samuel Pepys buried a wheel of cheese to protect it from the fire!

THE *TITANIC*

WHEN: **1912** WHERE: **North Atlantic Ocean**

The *Titanic* was carrying about 2,200 people from England to the United States on what turned out to be its first and only trip. Late one night, the *Titanic* hit an iceberg and started to sink.

Sadly, there were not enough lifeboats for everyone. Many passengers ended up in the extremely cold water. Some were rescued, but most of them froze to death.

More than 1,500 people died when the *Titanic* sank.

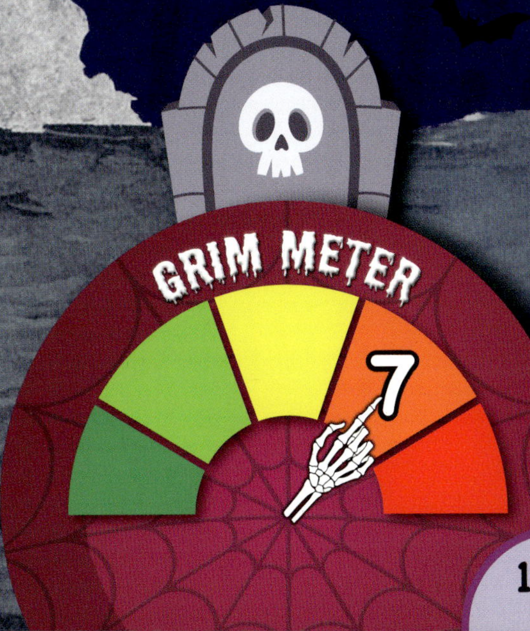

CHERNOBYL

WHEN: **1986** WHERE: **Pryp'yat, Ukraine**

During what was supposed to be a safety test, the Chernobyl **nuclear** power plant exploded. It sent out waves of **radioactive** materials. Within weeks, 30 workers had died from this deadly accident.

But the disaster didn't end there. The radioactive material continued to cause health problems and painful deaths for those people who were exposed to it. Today, it is still very dangerous to go near what is left of the plant.

DANGER

RADIOACTIVE MATERIALS

Scientists say it will take thousands of years for the area around Chernobyl to be safe again.

An abandoned park near Chernobyl

THE SAN FRANCISCO EARTHQUAKE

WHEN: **1906** WHERE: **San Francisco, California**

Around 5 a.m., a big earthquake hit the San Francisco area. The shaking was so strong that people felt it hundreds of miles away.

Soon after, deadly fires broke out across the damaged city. For days, the fires burned while the city continued to be hit with **aftershocks**. Over the course of the disaster, more than 3,000 people died.

This earthquake was one of the deadliest in the history of the United States.

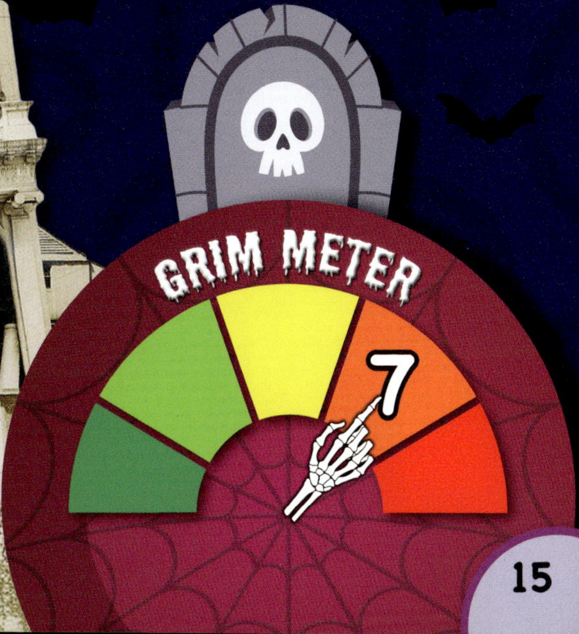

POMPEII

WHEN: **79 CE** WHERE: **Pompeii, Italy**

Throughout history, Mount Vesuvius has erupted many times. But one day, it did more than spew a little lava and poisonous gas . . . It destroyed the entire city of Pompeii!

Some of the shapes of the bodies of people who died during the eruption appear frozen in time. They were **preserved** by the ash.

More than 2,000 people are thought to have died when Mount Vesuvius erupted. Most of them choked on the gases or were buried under ash. And nearly 2,000 years later, most of Pompeii is still buried.

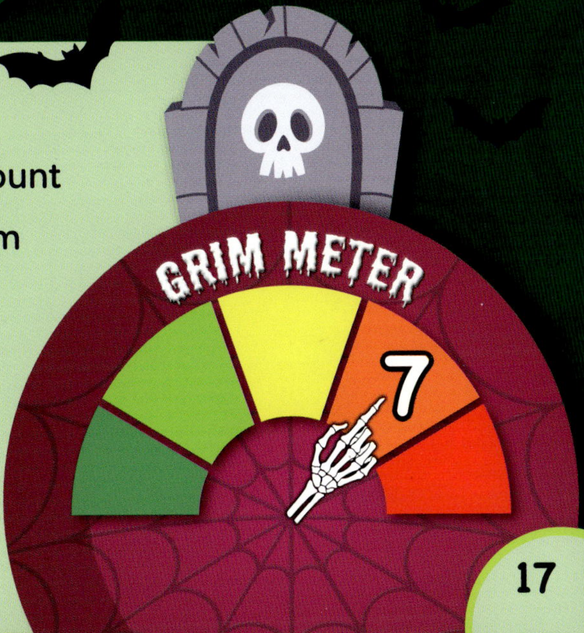

THE GALVESTON HURRICANE

WHEN: **1900** WHERE: **Galveston, Texas**

Two women search the remains of their home after the hurricane.

As a deadly hurricane hit the city of Galveston, the strong winds ripped buildings apart. Many people were swept out to sea.

HURRICANE ALERT!

Scientists knew this storm was coming, but they didn't know how powerful it would be.

At least 6,000 people died. There were too many bodies to bury on land so most were dumped back into the sea. Days later, many of them washed back up on shore.

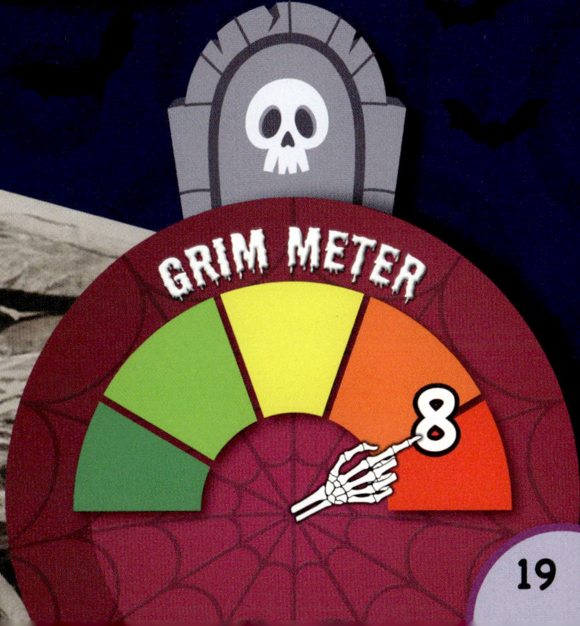

THE FRENCH REVOLUTION

WHEN: **1789** WHERE: **France**

King Louis XVI loved to spend money. He spent so much, he left France nearly broke. So, the king raised heavy **taxes** on the lower classes to get money back. This led the people to a **revolution**.

Maximilien Robespierre, who helped start the revolution, also ended up getting his head cut off!

Before the revolution, kings and queens would often **punish** people by cutting off their heads. So, the people did the same thing to them. This caused even more fighting over who would rule France. Soon, it seemed as if nearly everyone was getting their head chopped off!

THE BLACK DEATH

WHEN: **1347–1351** WHERE: **Europe**

In medieval times, a deadly disease started to spread quickly through Europe. It caused the skin to swell and ooze pus and blood. This terrible plague was called the Black Death.

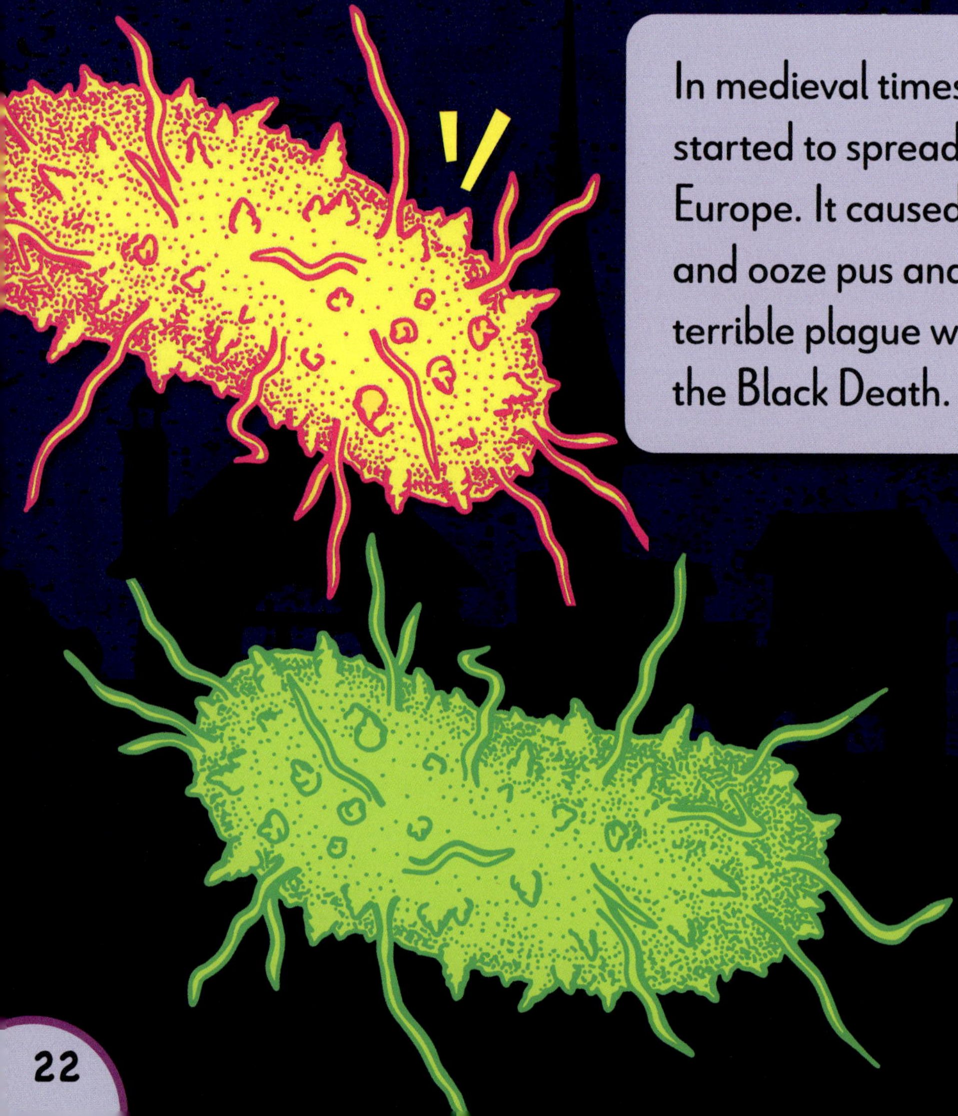

People tried to stop the sickness in many different ways. They rubbed themselves with onions, herbs, and dead pigeons. Some people drank poison while others drank pee! Unfortunately, none of these things helped.

The Black Death is thought to have killed at least 25 million people in 4 years!

GLOSSARY

abandoned empty or no longer used

aftershocks smaller earthquakes that happen after larger ones

nuclear having to do with a dangerous type of energy that produces radiation

plague a disease that causes death and spreads quickly

preserved kept in good condition

punish to get a penalty for a fault

radioactive giving off dangerous, invisible energy

revolution the attempt to overthrow a government

taxes money paid by people to the ruler of a country or the government

tribe a group of people who live together

INDEX